A First Guide to Grammar

by Jackie Eyles
Illustrated by Sonia Canals

Wayland

English Grammar

Start Right
A First Guide to Grammar

Get It Right
A Further Guide to Grammar

Editor: Katie Roden
Designer: Mark Whitchurch
Illustrator: Sonia Canals
Consultant: Ian Enters, English Adviser, Curriculum and Staff Development Service, Southfield Centre, Sheffield

First published in 1995 by
Wayland (Publishers) Ltd
61 Western Road, Hove,
East Sussex BN3 1JD, England

© Copyright 1995 Wayland (Publishers) Ltd

British Library Cataloguing in Publication Data
Eyles, Jackie
Start Right: First Guide to Grammar. –
(English Grammar Series)
I. Title II. Canals, Sonia III. Series
428.2

HARDBACK: ISBN 0-7502-1264-0

PAPERBACK: ISBN 0-7502-1710-3

Typeset by Mark Whitchurch
Printed and bound by Rotolito, Italy

National Curriculum Attainment Targets

The activities in this book focus on the requirements of the National Curriculum English document for Attainment Target 3: Writing. These cover levels 1-3 at Key Stage 1.

Children at KS1 should be able to:

- write each letter of the alphabet;
- learn simple spelling patterns;
- write common letter strings;
- spell commonly occurring simple words;
- construct and convey ideas in a variety of forms for different purposes;
- show knowledge of simple spelling conventions and accuracy in the punctuation of a sentence.

These skills are developed throughout the book.

Contents

Introduction	4
The alphabet	6
Words	10
Sentences	18
Glossary	30
Books to read	31
Notes for parents and teachers	31
Index	32

These words tell you what is in the book.

These numbers tell you what page things are on.

Words in **bold** are explained in the glossary on page 30.

CHAPTER 1 — Introduction

This is Bookworm.

This book is all about **grammar** and how to use it. It will help you to say and write anything you want – stories for your friends, cards and **invitations** and even a **dictionary**! Bookworm and Leapfrog will help you to do this.

Chapter 2: The alphabet

Everything you say or write is made up of **letters**. These letters are arranged in an order called the **alphabet**.

There are 26 letters in the English alphabet:

Make an alphabet frieze

Write each letter on a big piece of paper, like this.

Now think of a word that starts with that letter, like 'aeroplane' for the letter a.

Do this for all the letters, and stick them around the wall in the right order.

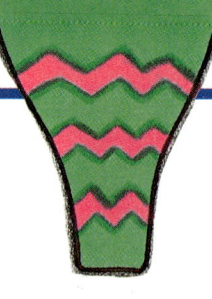

Chapter 3

When you put letters together, you can make **words**. Words help you to describe all the things you think, feel and see.

It's easy to make words if you know how.

Words that sound the same often use the same letters.

cat

mat

hat

dog

log

frog

That's me!

shop **sh**ip **sh**ell

p**ea** t**ea** s**ea**

Some words can tell you where things are.

Some words are doing words, called **verbs**. They help you to describe things that happen.

Leapfrog and Bookworm **eat** ice cream.

Leapfrog **swims** in the sea.

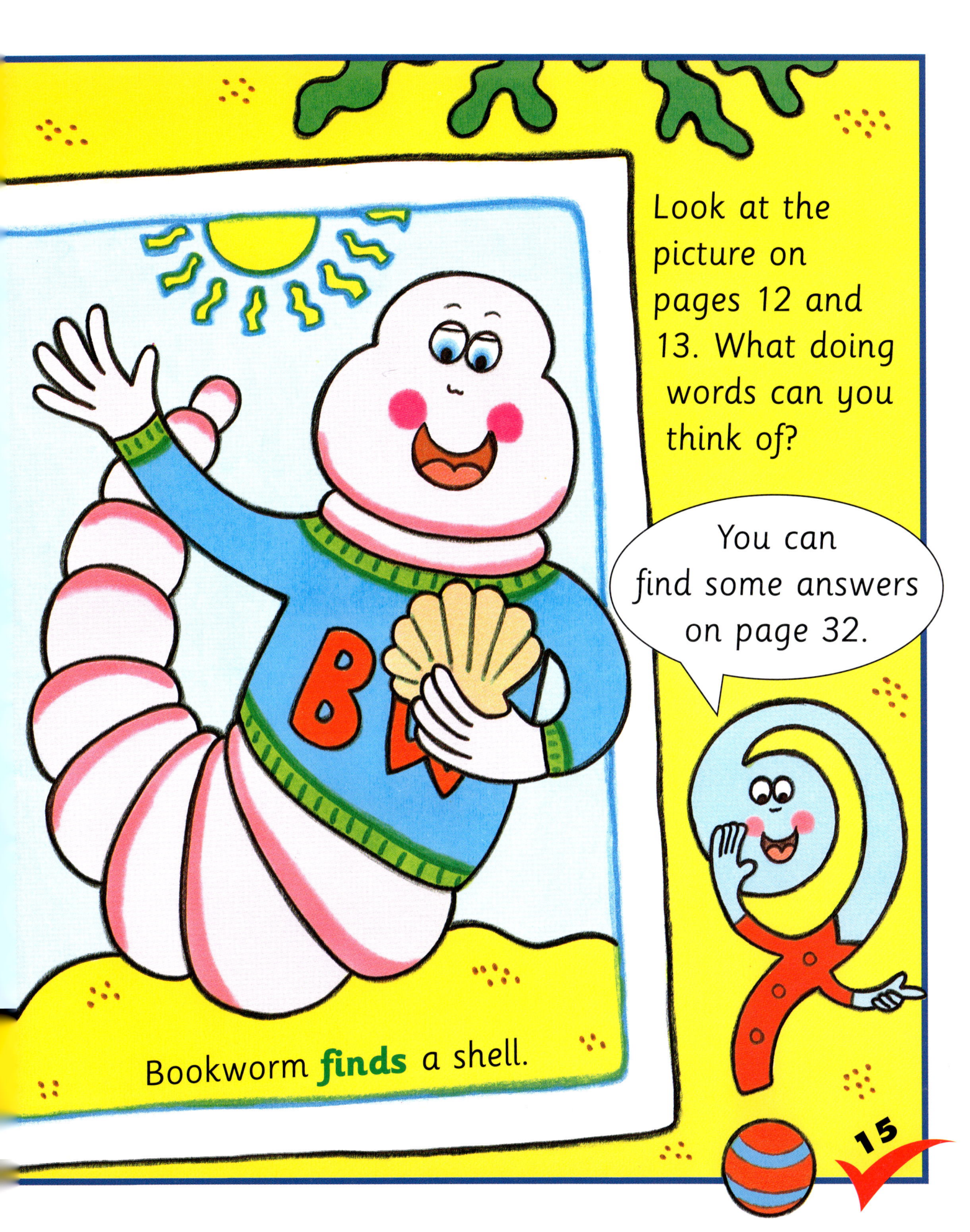

Bookworm **finds** a shell.

Look at the picture on pages 12 and 13. What doing words can you think of?

You can find some answers on page 32.

Write the alphabet in the book, with one letter at the top of each page. When you learn a new word, put it on the page with the first letter of the word at the top, and draw a picture to describe it.

CHAPTER 4 Sentences

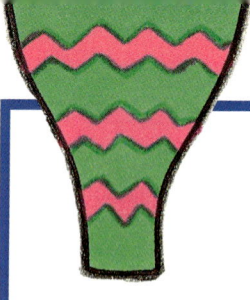

When you speak and write, you always use **sentences**. In a sentence, you need spaces between words so that you can understand it.

Yesterday we went to the beach.

Weswamintheseaandatesomeicecream.

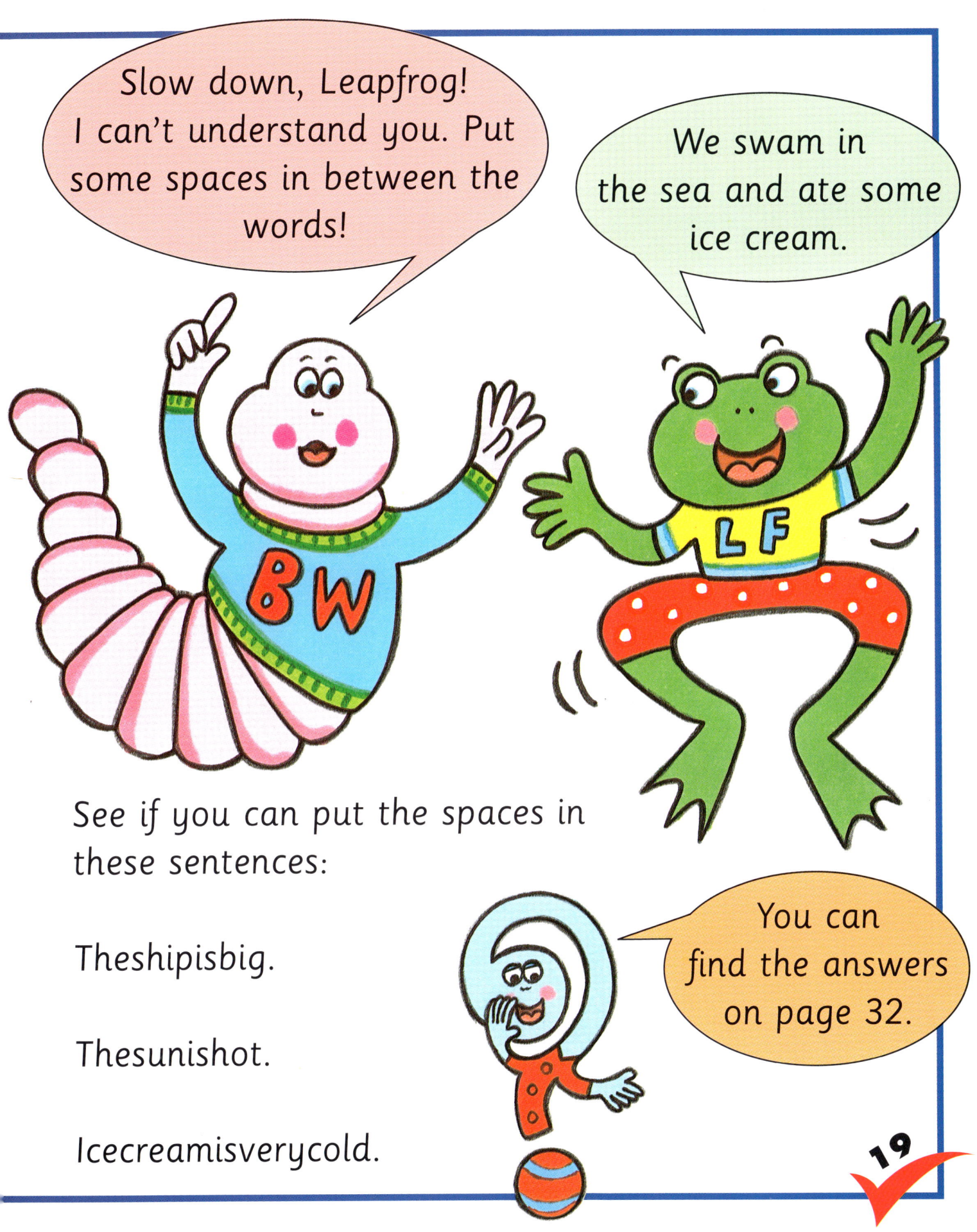

"Slow down, Leapfrog! I can't understand you. Put some spaces in between the words!"

"We swam in the sea and ate some ice cream."

See if you can put the spaces in these sentences:

Theshipisbig.

Thesunishot.

Icecreamisverycold.

"You can find the answers on page 32."

Another way of making your sentences clear is by using **capital letters** and **full stops**.

Start a sentence with a capital letter. These are big versions of the letters of the alphabet:

Rr Ss Tt Uu

Vv Ww Xx

Yy Zz

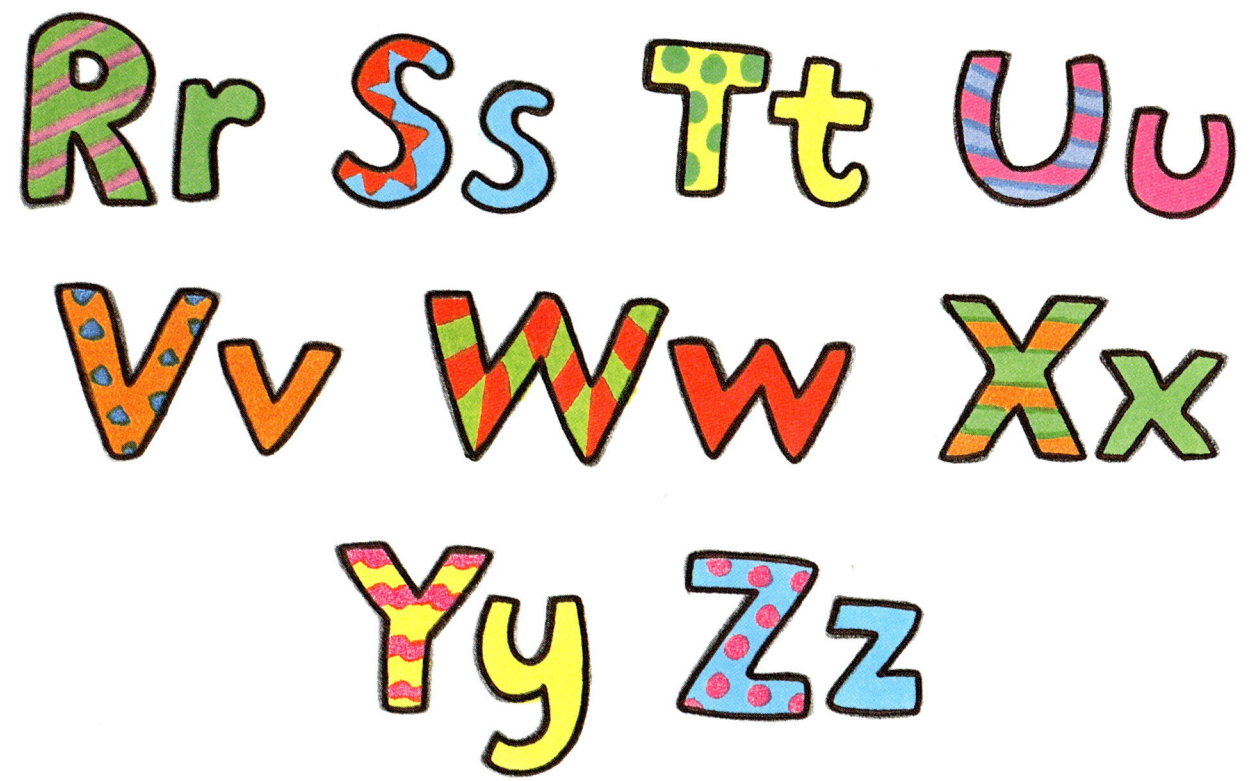

Add these to your alphabet frieze.

End a sentence with a full stop.
This tells you when to take a
breath as you read.

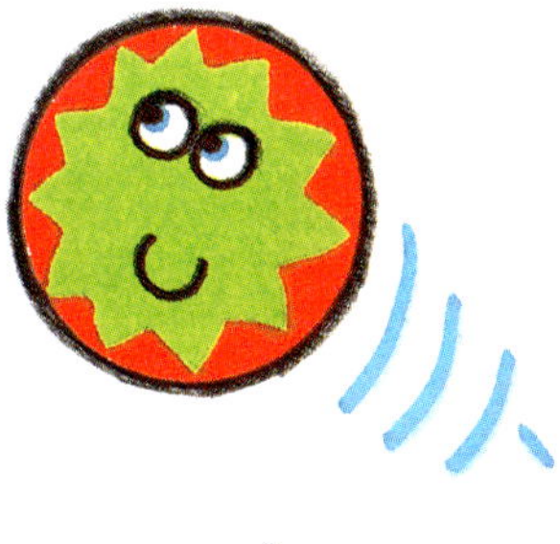

Now you can write lots of sentences in a row.

We went to the beach**.** **W**e swam in the sea**.**
We ate some ice cream**.**

It's my birthday! I'm having a party at the zoo! I need to make invitations to ask my friends to come. But how do I write them?

On the invitations, you must say the name of the person, the day of the party, the time it starts and where it is.

Names and places always start with a capital letter.

Days of the week also start with a capital letter.

Leapfrog invites Bookworm to a birthday party at 4'o'clock on Friday at Riverbank Zoo, Saint Kermit's Lane, Ribbitton, Croakshire.

You can make cards for lots of special days, such as Christmas, Diwali, weddings – or just to be friendly.

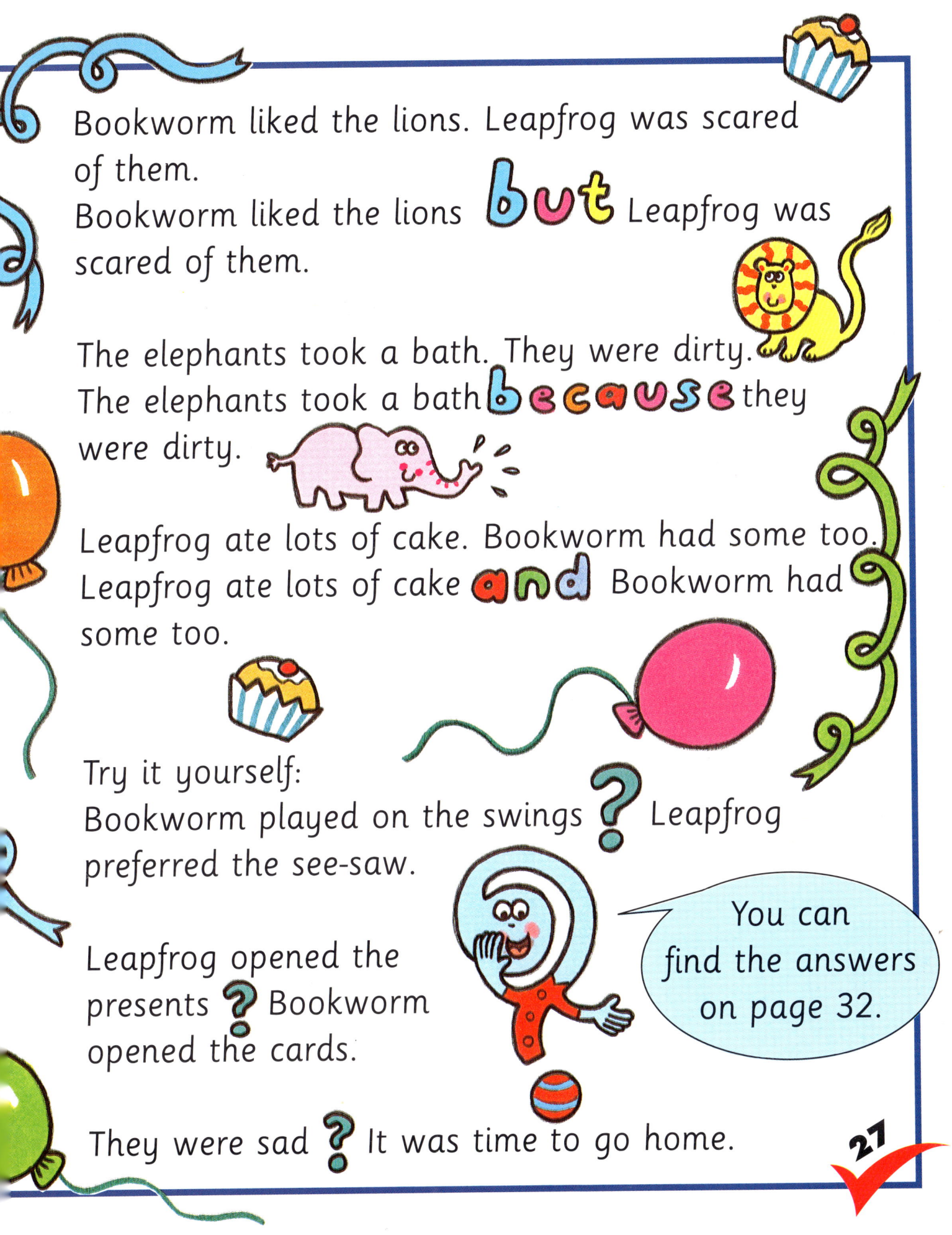

Bookworm liked the lions. Leapfrog was scared of them.
Bookworm liked the lions **but** Leapfrog was scared of them.

The elephants took a bath. They were dirty.
The elephants took a bath **because** they were dirty.

Leapfrog ate lots of cake. Bookworm had some too.
Leapfrog ate lots of cake **and** Bookworm had some too.

Try it yourself:
Bookworm played on the swings **?** Leapfrog preferred the see-saw.

Leapfrog opened the presents **?** Bookworm opened the cards.

They were sad **?** It was time to go home.

You can find the answers on page 32.

Now you know how to write sentences, you can write stories. Try writing a story about Bookworm and Leapfrog, following these pictures.

Why not write a book of stories with your friends? Your stories can be about Leapfrog and Bookworm or about anything you like! Draw lots of pictures to go with your stories.

Glossary

alphabet Twenty-six letters used for making words.

capital letters The big letters used at the beginning of a sentence and for special words.

dictionary A book of words with meanings. The words are arranged in the order of the alphabet.

full stops The marks used for finishing a sentence.

grammar A system which helps us to learn, speak and write our languages.

invitations Cards inviting someone to a special occasion.

joining words Words that make two or more sentences into one sentence.

letters The symbols that make up the alphabet.

sentences Sets of words that make sense when they are put together.

verbs Words that describe actions.

words Groups of letters. Each word has a different meaning.

Books to read

All About English by John and Elizabeth Seely (Oxford Primary Books, 1990)

English 7-12 (series) by D. Hughes and A. Josephs (Collins, 1993)

English Links (series) by Sheila Lane and Marion Kemp (Collins, 1992)

Practice in the Basic Skills – English (series) by D. Newton and D. Smith (Collins, 1993)

The Usborne Book of English Grammar by R. Gee and C. Watson (Usborne, 1983)

Word Patterns (series) by Peter and Joan Moss (Collins, 1988)

Notes for parents and teachers

Reading and writing are essential skills that children need to develop. They are the tools for learning in all other areas of the school curriculum and for learning at home. This book can be used at school and at home and has been designed to help children enjoy reading and writing. A wide range of activities will give children the confidence to become fluent readers and writers.

Start Right has pages of fun activities that will develop writing skills. It should be shared with parents and teachers so that a partnership of learning is developed. The child should have a book with pages of plain paper in which to do the activities and access to a range of materials for making cards, invitations, pictures etc.

Index

alphabet 6-9, 17

capital letters 20-1, 22
cards 5, 23

dictionaries 5, 16

full stops 20, 21

invitations 5, 22

joining words 26-7

languages 9
letters 6-9, 10, 17

sentences 18-21, 24-7, 28
stories 5, 28-9

verbs 14-15

words 10-17

Answers

page 13 You might have found: The sun in the sky. Bookworm on a post. A basket full of shells. A seagull in the sky. An apple in the sand.

page 15 Leapfrog **holds** a bucket. Leapfrog **digs** in the sand. The girl **reads** her book. The ship **sails** on the sea. The sun **shines** brightly. The seagull **flies** in the sky.

page 19 The ship is big. The sun is hot. Ice cream is very cold.

page 27 Bookworm played on the swings **but** Leapfrog preferred the see-saw.
Leapfrog opened the presents **and** Bookworm opened the cards.
They were sad **because** it was time to go home.

Did you get the answers right?